A Basket of Plums

A Basket of Plums

SONGS IN THE TRADITION OF
THICH NHAT HANH

PARALLAX PRESS
BERKELEY, CA

Parallax Press
P.O. Box 7355
Berkeley, California 94707

Parallax Press is the publishing division of
Unified Buddhist Church, Inc.
© 2009 by Unified Buddhist Church.
All rights reserved.
Printed in China.

Illustrations on pages 2, 6, 10, 12, 13, 19, 24, 29, 30, 35, 37, 48, 49, 50, 52, 53 by Wietske Vriezen. All other drawings by members of the Plum Village community.

Cover and text design by Debbie Berne
www.debbiebernedesign.com

For copyright information contact Parallax Press.

songs

BASKET OF PLUMS I

Happiness Is Here and Now 12
Island of the Self 13
The Moon 14
The Rain 16
Song of the Wind 17
Gathas for Mindful Eating 18
Here Is the Pure Land 19
No Coming, No Going 20
Watch the Rosebud Open 20
Gatha for Planting a Tree 21
Breathe, You Are Alive 22
Please Call Me by My True Names 23
Winter Song 24
Hy's Song 25
Awareness Is a Mirror 26
And When I Rise 27
Breathing In, Breathing Out 28
In, Out, Deep, Slow 29
Realm of the Mind 30
Honey in Your Eyes 31

BASKET OF PLUMS II

Happiness Makes You Beautiful 32
Simple Gifts 33
Let the Buddha Walk with You 34
I Hold the Earth and the Sky 36
Mealtime Meditation 37
Garden Hymn 38
Peace Is Every Step 39
How Can I Keep from Singing 40
There Is No Need 41
Namo Buddhaya 41
I Learn Each Moment 42
I Have Arrived 42
Compassion Springs from the Heart 43
Guarding the Six Senses 44
In the Bleak Midwinter 46
See the Green Blade Rising 47
Reverence Is the Nature of My Love 48
Now I Walk in Beauty 49
The River and the Sky 50
Earthsong 51
My Head Resting on Waves 52

foreword

Speaking with loving kindness and listening deeply and with compassion is an art. When you sing a song, the song should have an effect of creating beauty, of building mutual understanding and compassion. That's what we try to do in our community. We write poetry, we write songs, we perform dances, and we chant. Everything we do is to help introduce more harmony into our Sangha, our community. Slowly, we become brothers and sisters to each other. Without community, we cannot go far.

When I invite the bell, I am playing music. This music is wonderful, because it brings calm and peace to you and to the whole community. I have been practicing listening to the bell and inviting the bell all my life and, until one night when I dreamed about it, had not realized that I was practicing music. The bell, like these songs, is the kind of spiritual music that facilitates mutual understanding and happiness in people.

I am convinced that each of us has a bell in our pockets. We can all be students of music. Our bodies and minds will sing with joy. We have not just one but many musical instruments. Our in-breath and out-breath are a kind of violin that we can play all day. Our steps, our lungs, our noses—everything can become a musical instrument. We can play music while sitting, walking, or eating. And as I am a student of music, I invite all of you to be my co-students, and you will learn how to play music in such a way that will bring peace to our society, our communities, and ourselves.

THICH NHAT HANH

introduction

Dharma songs are Dharma talks in miniature. For Thich Nhat Hanh, a Dharma talk is not a lecture, but a kind of rain. "Our consciousness is like the soil, the earth. We have to allow the Dharma talk to penetrate it. According to the Buddha, we have seeds of understanding, of awakening, and of compassion within ourselves. We don't need these seeds to be transmitted from a teacher. We already have all of them in the depth of our consciousness. Because these seeds may be buried deep in the mind, in the soil of our consciousness, it is hard for them to grow and manifest. Above them there are layers of suffering, confusion and prejudice, and our intellect alone can never go deep enough."

Sr. Annabel Laity captures the essence of Thich Nhat Hanh's meaning in her song "The Rain," which was written while taking shelter from a rainstorm in the Upper Hamlet of Plum Village. All the songs in this collection aspire to be the kind of Dharma rain that waters the positive seeds that bring us and others happiness.

The song "I Have Arrived" is the theme song of Plum Village, or in Thich Nhat Hanh's words, it is "the seal of Plum Village. Any practice that does not include this, or is contrary to its spirit, is not Plum Village practice." Hardly a day passes at Plum Village when the Sangha doesn't sing this song.

On June 8, 2002, during the Hand of the Buddha retreat, Thich Nhat Hanh shared the profound meaning that music has for him: "When the Sangha comes together, the deep mindful breathing is music. We enjoy this music very much. There are times when we sit together and don't do anything. We don't work hard at all. We just produce our being, our full presence, and become aware of the Sangha. That is enough to nourish and heal us. If you know how to allow yourself to be embraced by the Sangha, to become the Sangha, to be penetrated by the music of the Sangha, then transformation and healing can take place already. Music sometimes can be very silent. It can create harmony. It can calm things down. It can heal."

These songs are healing songs. They sing of the wholeness of the self, the wholeness of the community, and the wholeness of nature. They point to this wholeness for a brief moment, remind us of our insights and vows, and turn the silence that follows into practice.

JOSEPH EMET, COLLECTOR AND SONGWRITER

songs

Island of the Self

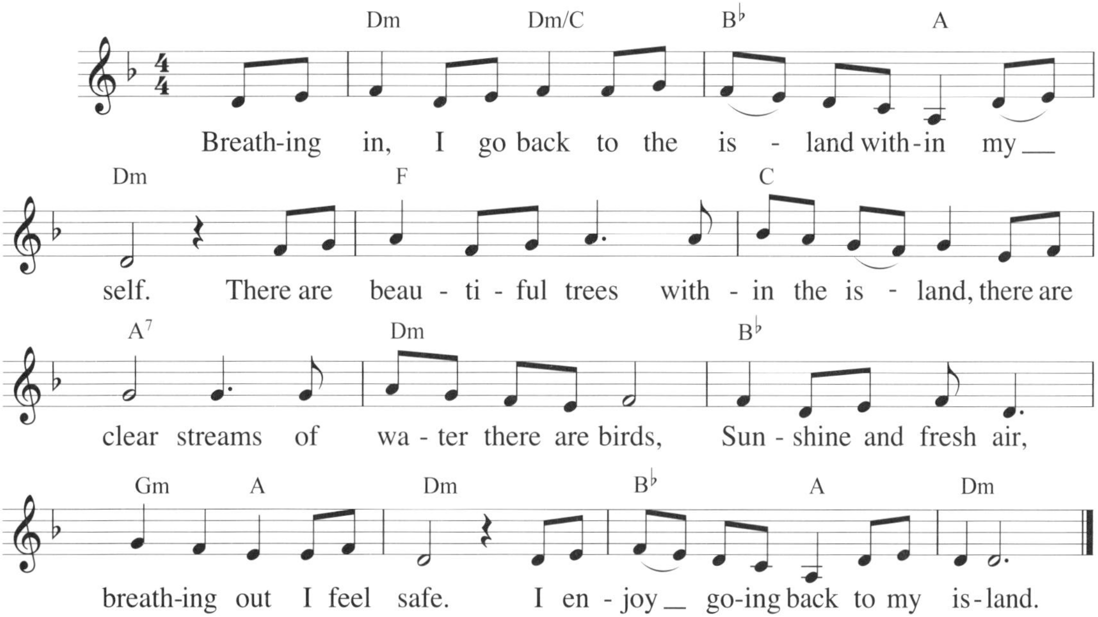
Dm Dm/C B♭ A
Breath-ing in, I go back to the is - land with-in my
Dm F C
self. There are beau - ti - ful trees with - in the is - land, there are
A7 Dm B♭
clear streams of wa - ter there are birds, Sun - shine and fresh air,
Gm A Dm B♭ A Dm
breath-ing out I feel safe. I en - joy go-ing back to my is-land.

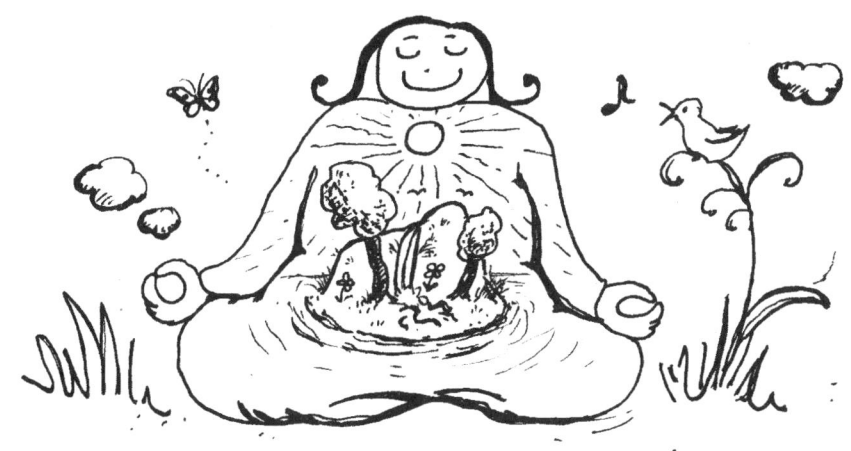

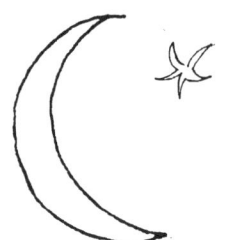

The Moon

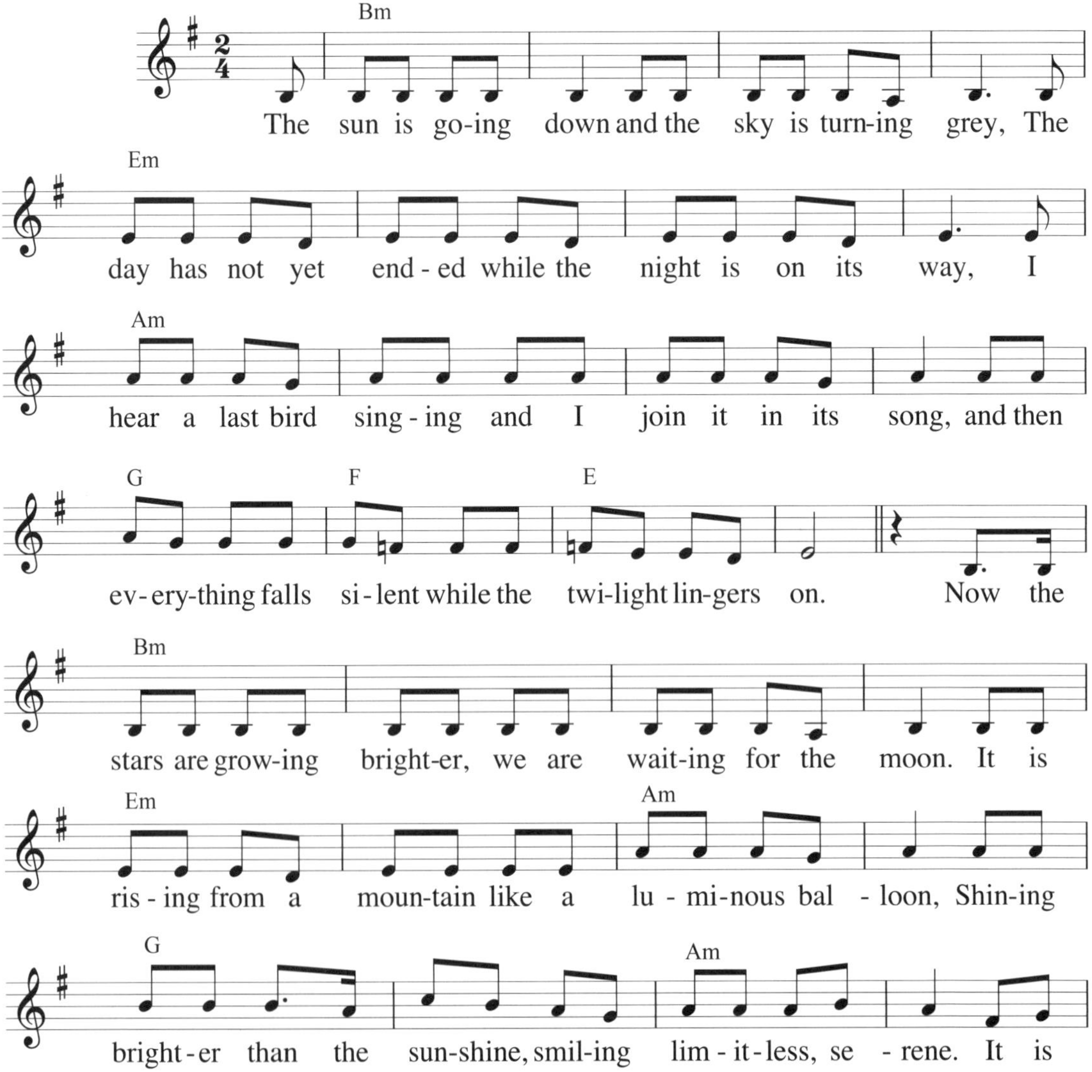
Bm
The sun is go-ing down and the sky is turn-ing grey, The
Em
day has not yet end - ed while the night is on its way, I
Am
hear a last bird sing - ing and I join it in its song, and then
G F E
ev - ery-thing falls si - lent while the twi-light lin-gers on. Now the
Bm
stars are grow-ing bright-er, we are wait-ing for the moon. It is
Em Am
ris - ing from a moun-tain like a lu - mi-nous bal - loon, Shin-ing
G Am
bright - er than the sun-shine, smil-ing lim - it - less, se - rene. It is

The Rain

Song of the Wind

I lis-ten to the song of the wind it has no name, — I
lis-ten to the song of the wind it has no words, _____ I
lis-ten to the song of the wind and I can see: _____ The
wind is free. _____ The wind is free. _____
We are the wind, _____ and we are free. _____

Gathas for Mindful Eating

Here Is the Pure Land

No Coming, No Going

Watch the Rosebud Open

Please Call Me by My True Names

Winter Song

The gift of a qui-et mind brings us peace and heal-ing, the gift of a qui-et heart makes love sweet; Win-ning or los-ing, peace-ful-ly breath-ing, Watch-ing the snow fall on cat's feet.

Hy's Song

And When I Rise

Breathing In, Breathing Out

In, Out, Deep, Slow

In, out, deep _ slow; Calm, ease, smile, re - lease.
Pres - ent mo - ment, Won - der - ful mo - ment.

Realm of the Mind

The realm of the mind is mine I can choose. I can choose where I want to be. Both heav-en and hell, I know e-qual-ly well. The choice is up to me.

Honey in Your Eyes

Happiness Makes You Beautiful

Hap-pi-ness makes you beau-ti-ful, like a spring mead-ow in bloom, Where
Please walk with gen-tle-ness in a spring mead-ow in bloom, Where
daf-fo-dils and lil-ies grow, and grass-es sway with the breeze.
daf-fo-dils and lil-ies grow, and grass-es sway with the breeze. The
Hap-pi-ness is a flow-er that grows in a pure heart, En-
ten-der flower of happi-ness is more pre-cious than gold, En-
chant-ing all with its fra-grance, and sow-ing seeds in the wind.
chant-ing all with its fra-grance, and sow-ing seeds in the wind.

Let the Buddha Walk with You

bees are working in the garden, Working whole-heartedly, Like the butterflies, Gracefully, Let the Buddha work with you.

I Hold the Earth and the Sky

Mealtime Meditation

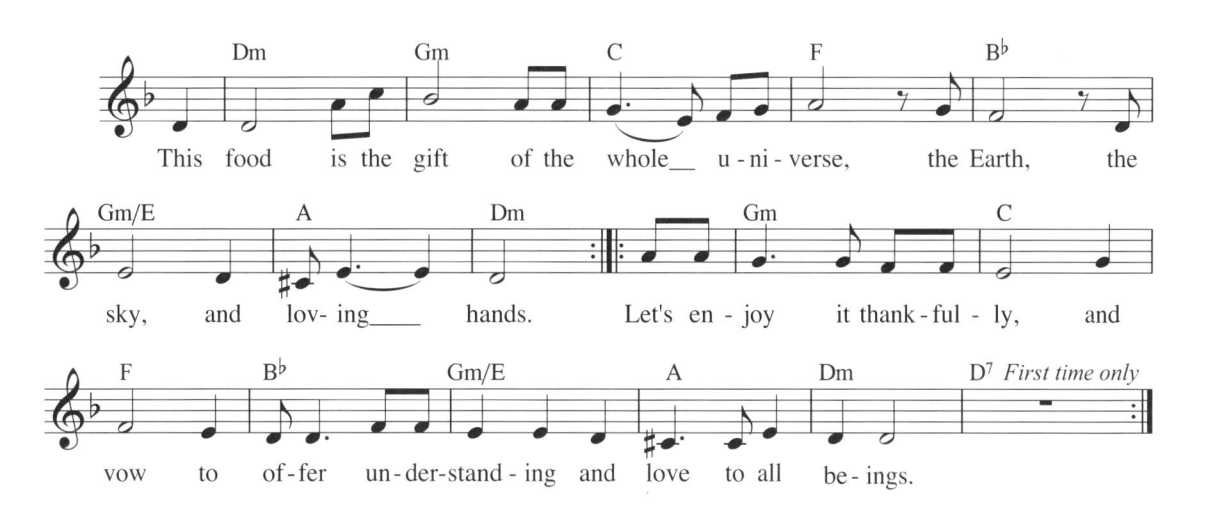

This food is the gift of the whole universe, the Earth, the sky, and loving hands. Let's enjoy it thankfully, and vow to offer understanding and love to all beings.

Garden Hymn

As I walk in Earth's green garden the spic-es yield a rich perfume, And the lil-ies grow and thrive, the lil-ies grow and thrive. I feel re-freshed with each breath, as I gaze with joy at ev-ery vine, And I ar-rive at home, And I ar-rive at home.

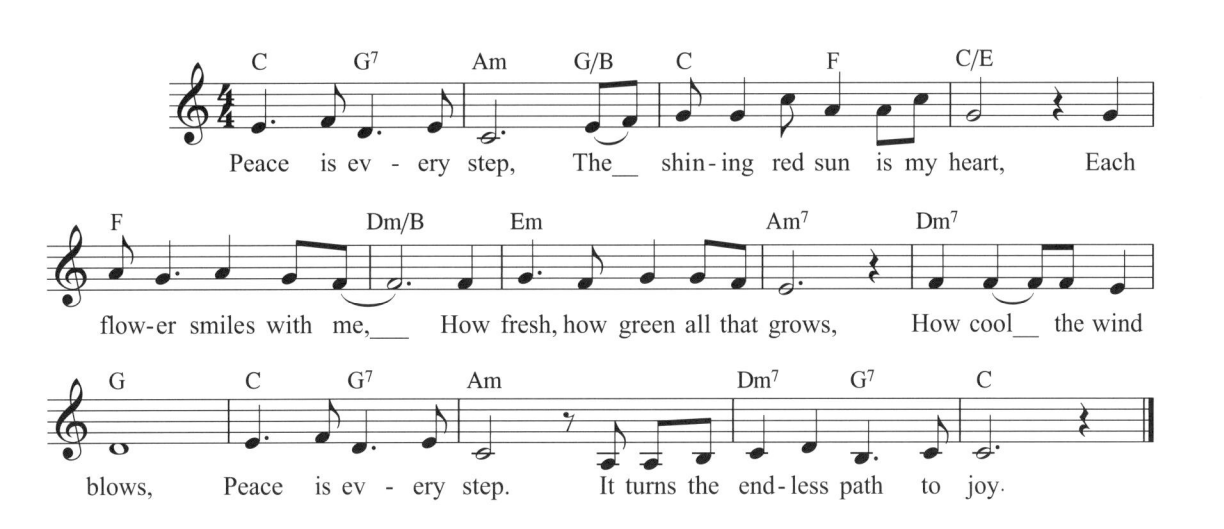

Peace Is Every Step

Peace is ev-ery step, The shin-ing red sun is my heart, Each flow-er smiles with me,___ How fresh, how green all that grows, How cool__ the wind blows, Peace is ev-ery step. It turns the end-less path to joy.

How Can I Keep from Singing

My life flows on in end - less song a - bove earth's la - men - ta - tion, I
Each time I see that through my fear, a peace - ful na - ture's shin - ing, With

hear a joy - ful mel - o - dy, that cuts through all af - flic - tion. _ Through
love of friends both near and far, how can I keep from sing - ing. _ The

all the tu - mult and the strife I hear that mu - sic ring - ing, _ It
storms don't shake me deep _ down while to that tune I'm lis - ten - ing, _ With

brings me joy with _ ev' - ry breath, how can I keep from sing - ing. _
love for all be - ings in my heart, how can I keep from sing - ing. _

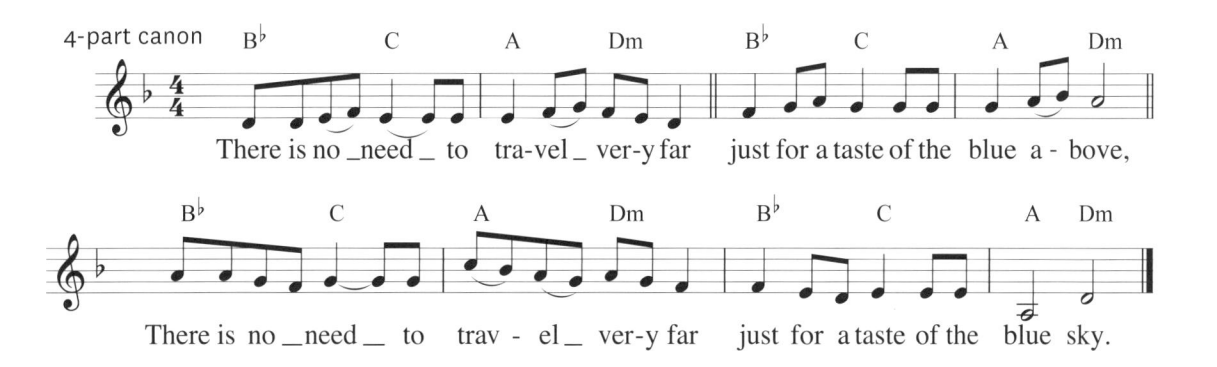

There Is No Need

4-part canon

There is no need to tra-vel ver-y far just for a taste of the blue a-bove,

There is no need to trav-el ver-y far just for a taste of the blue sky.

Namo Buddhaya

Na-mo Bud-dha-ya_____ Na-mo____ Bud-dha-ya, Na-mo Bud-dha-ya_____ Na-mo____ Bud-dha-ya, Na-mo____ Bud-dha-ya_____ Na-mo____ Bud-dha-ya, Na-mo____ Bud-dha-ya,_____ Na-mo Bud-dha-ya.

I Learn Each Moment

2-part round

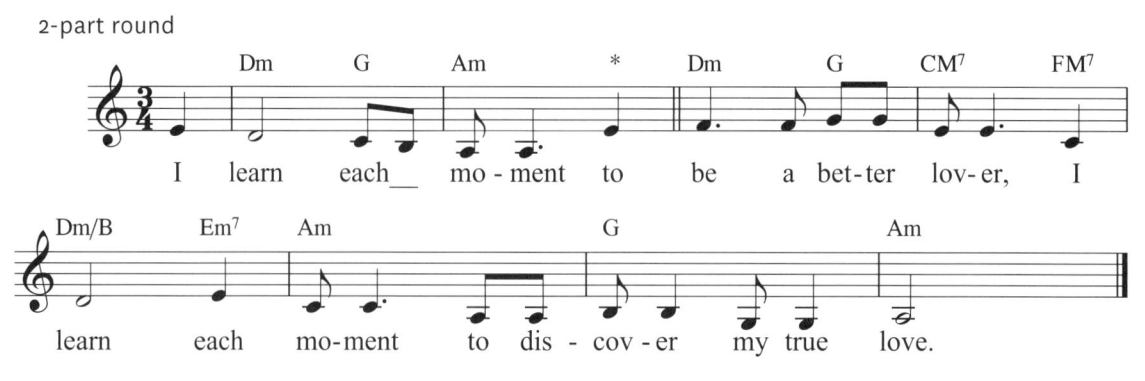

I learn each moment to be a better lover, I learn each moment to discover my true love.

*second voice enters

I Have Arrived

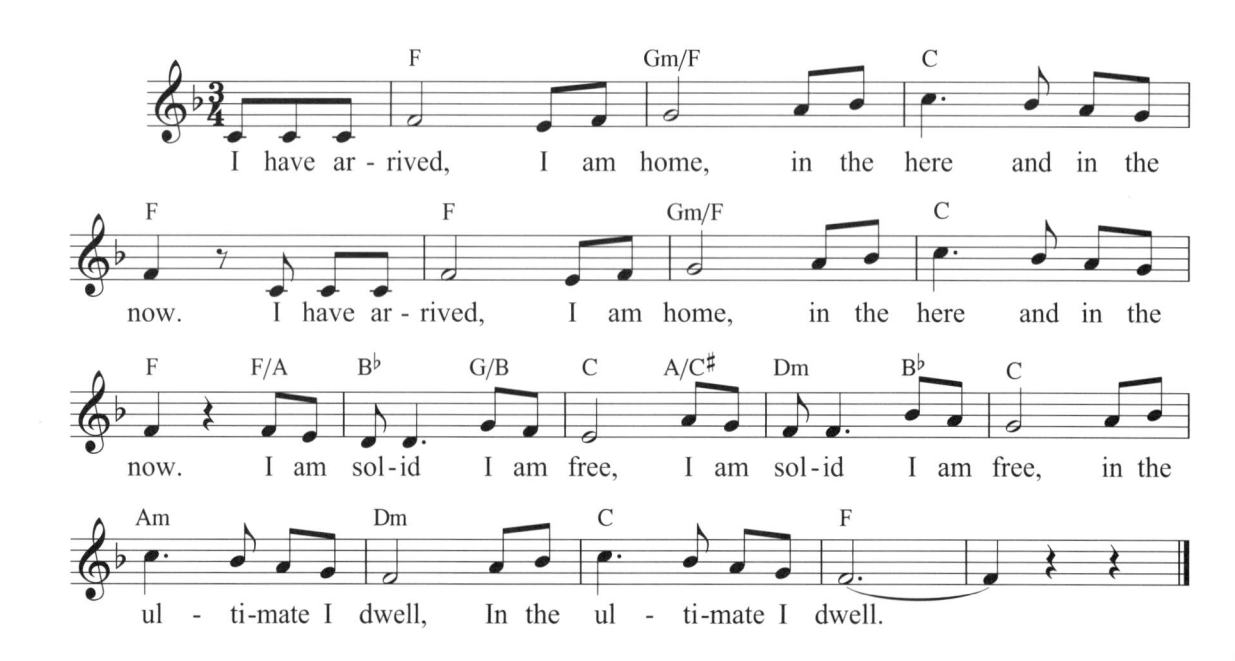

I have arrived, I am home, in the here and in the now. I have arrived, I am home, in the here and in the now. I am solid I am free, I am solid I am free, in the ultimate I dwell, In the ultimate I dwell.

Compassion Springs from the Heart

Com-pas-sion springs from the heart as pure, re-fresh-ing wa-ter,
Heal-ing the wounds of life, Turn-ing poi-son in - to flow-ers,
One flow-er, two flow-ers milli-ons of lit-tle flow-ers ap-pear in the fields, and weap-ons turn to dust. From the high-est peak of the moun-tain the bles-sed wa-ter, comes stream-ing down, comes stream-ing down, pen-e-trat-ing rice fields, and or-ange groves, The heal-ing wa-ter is the same on a wil-low branch, or in the heart, The leaves are still green, and the sun-light smiles on the snow.

Guarding the Six Senses

The eyes are a deep ocean, with whirlpools and violent winds, and shadows beneath the surface, and sea monsters deep within. My boat sails in mindfulness, I vow to hold the till-er firm-ly, ___ so I do not drown in an o-cean of form. Us-ing my con-scious breath, I am guard-ing my eyes For my pro-tec-tion ___ and yours. So that to-day ___ con-tin-ues __ to be a beau-ti-ful day, and to-mor-row, __ we still have each o-ther. _____ The ears an o-cean of sound, The tongue an o-cean of taste, The nose an o-cean of smell, And the mind an o-cean of dhar-mas.

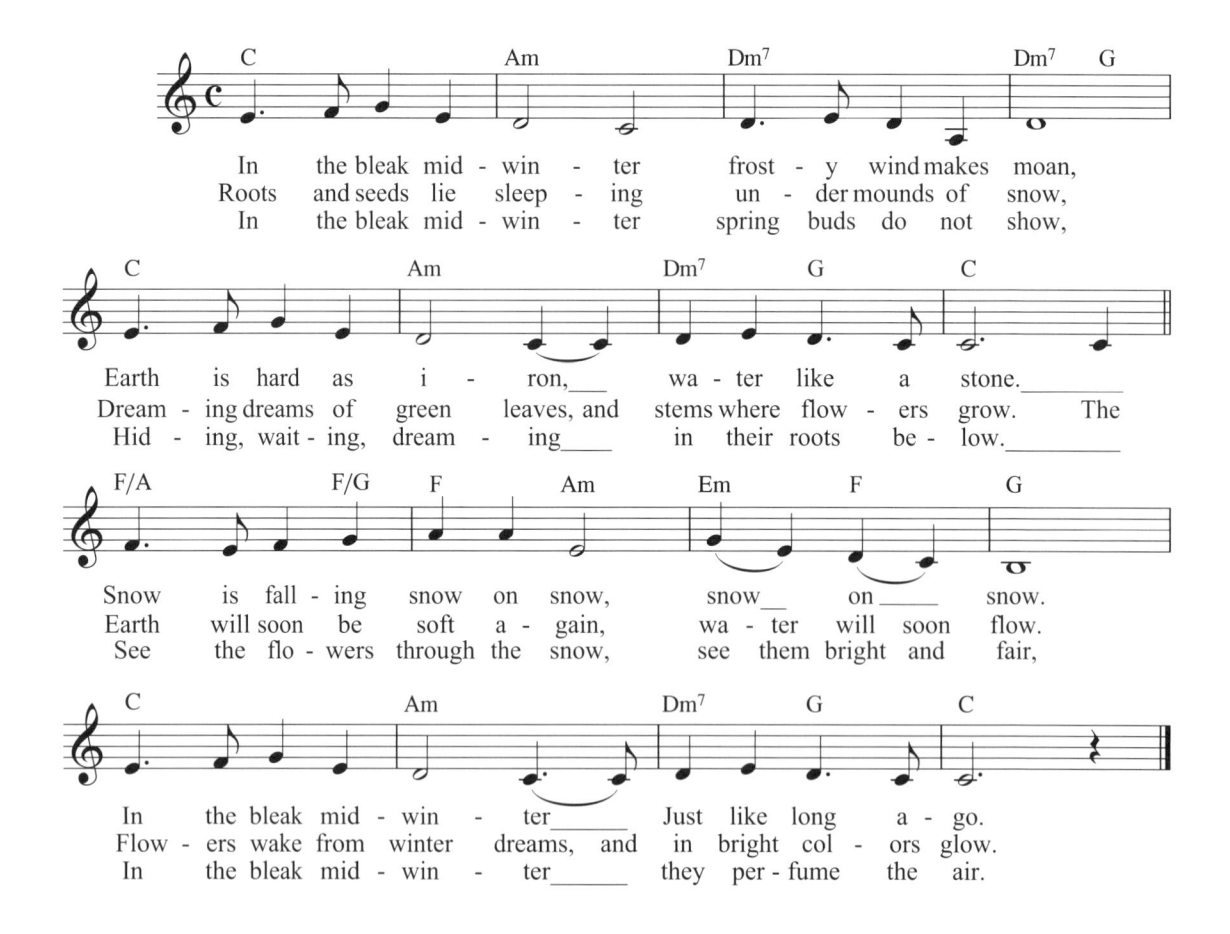

In the Bleak Midwinter

In the bleak mid-win-ter frost-y wind makes moan,
Roots and seeds lie sleep-ing un-der mounds of snow,
In the bleak mid-win-ter spring buds do not show,

Earth is hard as i-ron, wa-ter like a stone.
Dream-ing dreams of green leaves, and stems where flow-ers grow. The
Hid-ing, wait-ing, dream-ing in their roots be-low.

Snow is fall-ing snow on snow, snow on snow.
Earth will soon be soft a-gain, wa-ter will soon flow.
See the flo-wers through the snow, see them bright and fair,

In the bleak mid-win-ter Just like long a-go.
Flow-ers wake from winter dreams, and in bright col-ors glow.
In the bleak mid-win-ter they per-fume the air.

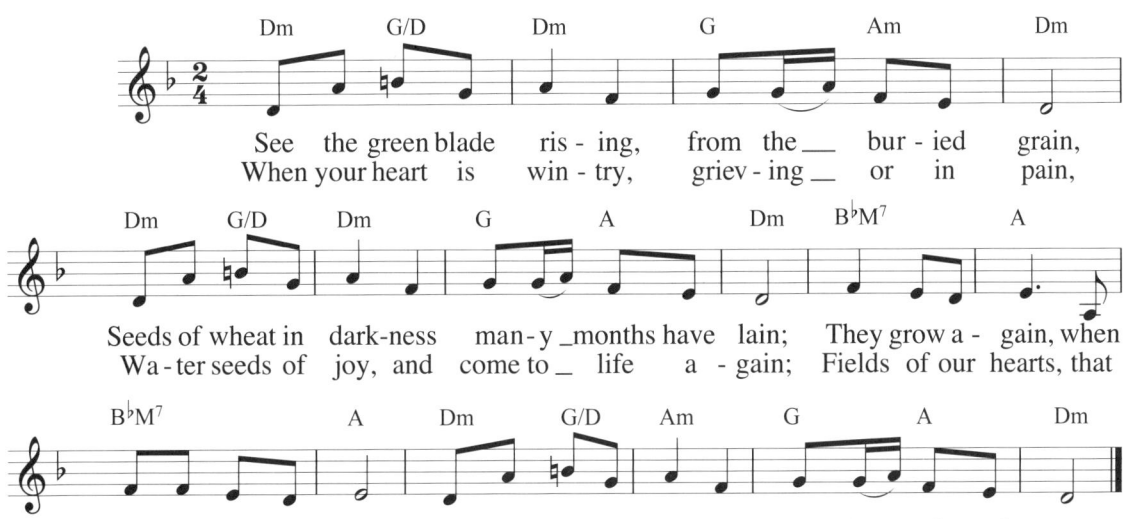

See the Green Blade Rising

See the green blade ris-ing, from the bur-ied grain,
Seeds of wheat in dark-ness man-y months have lain; They grow a-gain, when
wa-tered by the rain; Joy can rise a-gain like wheat that spring-eth green.

When your heart is win-try, griev-ing or in pain,
Wa-ter seeds of joy, and come to life a-gain; Fields of our hearts, that
cold and bare have been; Grow and thrive a-gain like wheat that spring-eth green.

Reverence Is the Nature of My Love

Rev-er-ence is the na-ture of my love, my love,
Rev-er-ence is the na-ture of my love I bow to the
bush-es, I bow to the flow-ers, I bow to the sing-ing birds in the
trees, I bow to the moun-tains, I bow to the
riv-ers, I bow to the danc-ing bees.

Now I Walk in Beauty

Now I walk in beauty, Beauty is before me,
I sit at beauty's table, Beauty's in the food before me,
I lie in beauty's cradle, Beauty's in the moon above,

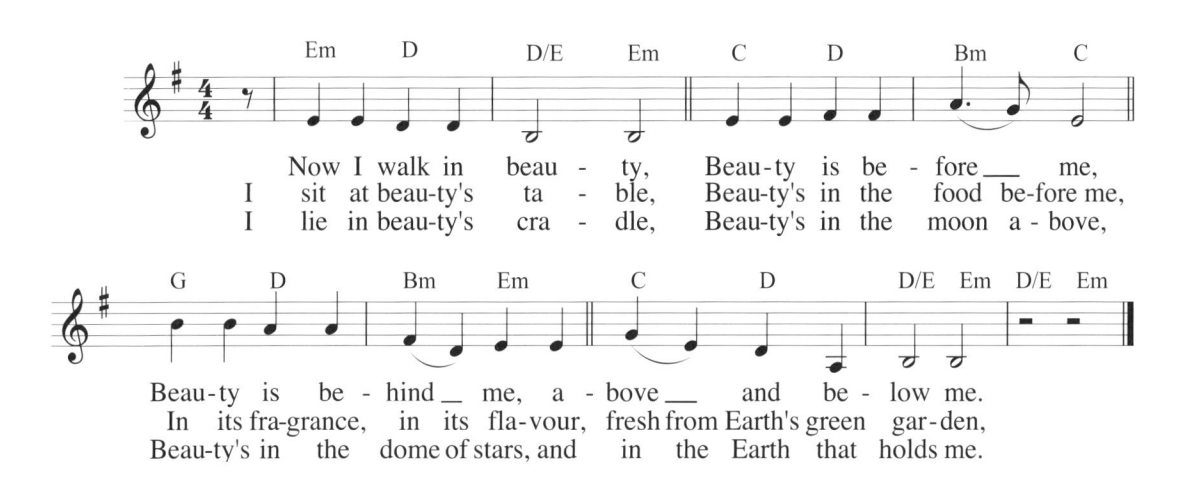

Beauty is behind me, above and below me.
In its fragrance, in its flavour, fresh from Earth's green garden,
Beauty's in the dome of stars, and in the Earth that holds me.

The River and the Sky

The riv-er and the sky are sing-ing a Dhar-ma song. Sing-ing and lis-tening be-come one, as a spar-row joins their song. Sing like the spar-row, lis-ten like the sky, for all is listen-ing, all is song. Sing like the spar-row, lis-ten like the sky, for sing-ing and listen-ing are al-rea-dy one.

Earthsong

I live on a mountain, I live by the sea, I live in a valley, I live by a stream, I live on the Earth, the Earth is my home, the home of my body the home of my mind
The wind blows through grasses, the wind blows through trees, My breath is a wind, that blows through me, The eyes in the sky, the eyes of awareness, the sun by day, the moon by night, the night in my arms.
This is my song, a love song for Earth, The Earth in my bowl the Earth in my cup, The Earth in my arms, I hold you with love, I hold the day, I hold the night, the night in my arms.

My Head Resting on Waves

My head rest-ing__ on waves, I drift with the flow. Broad riv-er deep sky,__ They float they sink, like bub-bles, like wings, Like bub-bles like wings. My head rest-ing__ on waves, I drift with the flow. Broad riv-er, deep sky__ They float, they sink, like bub-bles like wings, Like bub-bles like wings.

music credits

All words and music by Joseph Emet except where noted below.

Basket of Plums I

p12/Happiness Is Here and Now
Words and music: Evelyn Beumkes.

p13/Island of the Self
Words: Thich Nhat Hanh.
Music: Joseph Emet.

p14/The Moon
Words and music: Evelyn Beumkes.

p16/The Rain
Words and music: Sr. Annabel Laity.

p17/Song of the Wind
Words and music: Evelyn Beumkes.

p18/Gathas for Mindful Eating
Words: Thich Nhat Hanh.
Music: Sr. Annabel Laity.

p19/Here Is the Pure Land
Words: Thich Nhat Hanh.
Music: Ellen Deimann.

p20/No Coming, No Going
Words and music: Sr. Annabel Laity.

p21/Gatha for Planting a Tree
Music: Chant from Gao Ming Temple.
Words: Thich Nhat Hanh.
Adapted by Joseph Emet.

p22/Breathe, You Are Alive
Words and music: Sr. Annabel Laity.

p23/Please Call Me by My True Names
Words: Thich Nhat Hanh.
Music: Joseph Emet.

p25/Hy's Song
Words: Thich Nhat Hanh.
Music: Joseph Emet.

p26/Awareness Is a Mirror
Words: Thich Nhat Hanh.
Music: Michael Ciborski.

p27/And When I Rise
(For Charlie Malat)
Traditional song.
Adapted by Joseph Emet.

p28/Breathing In, Breathing Out
Words: Thich Nhat Hanh.
Music: Betsy Rose.

p29/In, Out, Deep, Slow
Words: Thich Nhat Hanh.
Music: Chan Hoa Lam.

p30/Realm of the Mind
Words and music: Evelyn Beumkes.

Vocals: Kerry-Ann Kutz, Jessica Vigneault, and Mai Nguyen. Arrangements, keyboards, flute, and Irish whistle: Joseph Emet. Violins: Shawn Yakimovitch and Jessica Gal. Sitar: Uwe Neumann. Organ: Christian Thomas. Bass: Eric Auclair. With Birds, Wind, and Rain.

Recorded by Christian Thomas.
Mixed by Francis Lelage.
Produced by Joseph Emet.

Basket of Plums II

p33/Simple Gifts
Traditional Shaker song.
Adapted by Joseph Emet.

p37/Mealtime Meditation
Words: Thich Nhat Hanh.
Adapted by Joseph Emet.

p38/Garden Hymn
Traditional southern hymn.
Adapted by Joseph Emet.

p39/Peace Is Every Step
Words: Thich Nhat Hanh.
Music: Joseph Emet.

p40/How Can I Keep from Singing
Traditional hymn.
Adapted by Joseph Emet.

p41/Namo Buddhaya
Words: Traditional Buddhist chant.
Music: Joseph Emet.

p42/I Learn Each Moment
Words: Thich Nhat Hanh.
Music: Joseph Emet.

p42/I Have Arrived
Traditional carol.
Words: Thich Nhat Hanh.

p43/Compassion Springs from the Heart
Words: Thich Nhat Hanh.
Music: Joseph Emet.

p44/Guarding the Six Senses
Words: Thich Nhat Hanh.
Music: Joseph Emet.

p46/In the Bleak Midwinter
Traditional carol.
Adapted by Joseph Emet.

p47/See the Green Blade Rising
Traditional May carol.
Adapted by Joseph Emet.

p48/Reverence Is the Nature of My Love
(For Michael and Fern)
Words adapted from Thich Nhat Hanh.
Music: Joseph Emet.

p49/Now I Walk in Beauty
(For Thay Giac Thanh)
Traditional song.
Adapted by Joseph Emet.

p52/My Head Resting on Waves
Words: Thich Nhat Hanh.
Music: Joseph Emet.

Vocals: Emily M. King.
Arrangements and keyboards: Joseph Emet.
Recorded and produced by Joseph Emet.

PARALLAX PRESS

Parallax Press, a nonprofit organization, publishes books on engaged Buddhism and the practice of mindfulness by Thich Nhat Hanh and other authors. All of Thich Nhat Hanh's work is available at our online store and in our free catalog. For a copy of the catalog, please contact:

Parallax Press
P.O. Box 7355
Berkeley, CA 94707
Tel: (510) 525-0101
www.parallax.org

Monastics and laypeople practice the art of mindful living in the tradition of Thich Nhat Hanh at retreat communities in France and the United States. To reach any of these communities, or for information about individuals and families joining for a practice period, please contact:

Plum Village	Blue Cliff Monastery	Deer Park Monastery
13 Martineau	3 Mindfulness Road	2499 Melru Lane
33580 Dieulivol, France	Pine Bush, NY 12566	Escondido, CA 92026
www.plumvillage.org	www.bluecliffmonastery.org	www.deerparkmonastery.org

The *Mindfulness Bell*, a journal of the art of mindful living in the tradition of Thich Nhat Hanh, is published three times a year by Plum Village. To subscribe or to see the worldwide directory of Sanghas, visit www.mindfulnessbell.org.